50 Beyond Eggs and Bacon Recipes for Home

By: Kelly Johnson

Table of Contents

- Avocado Toast with Cherry Tomatoes
- Quinoa Breakfast Bowl
- Chia Seed Pudding
- Smoothie Bowl with Granola
- Oatmeal with Fresh Fruit
- Banana Pancakes
- Greek Yogurt Parfait
- Breakfast Burrito with Veggies
- Sweet Potato Hash
- Muesli with Nuts and Dried Fruit
- Overnight Oats with Almond Butter
- Breakfast Tacos with Salsa
- Coconut Rice Pudding
- Berry Muffins
- Frittata with Spinach and Feta
- Smoothie with Spinach and Pineapple
- Savory Oatmeal with Cheese
- Tofu Scramble with Veggies
- Fruit Salad with Mint
- Whole Wheat Banana Bread
- Breakfast Quinoa with Maple Syrup
- Cinnamon Roll Overnight Oats
- Zucchini Fritters
- Almond Flour Waffles
- Rice Cakes with Nut Butter and Bananas
- Bagel with Lox and Cream Cheese
- Cauliflower Grits
- French Toast Casserole
- Polenta with Eggs and Tomato
- Savory Scones with Cheese and Chives
- Vegan Breakfast Bowl
- Puffed Rice with Dried Fruit
- Cornmeal Pancakes
- Apple Cinnamon Breakfast Bake
- Savory Oatmeal with Mushrooms

- Breakfast Couscous with Almonds
- Egg and Avocado Breakfast Sandwich
- Smoked Salmon and Avocado Salad
- Peanut Butter Banana Smoothie
- Berry Chia Jam on Toast
- Spinach and Mushroom Quiche
- Sweet Potato Pancakes
- Cacao Nib Granola
- Toasted Coconut Granola
- Matcha Overnight Oats
- Spicy Avocado Salsa on Toast
- Breakfast Ramen with Soft-Boiled Egg
- Ricotta and Honey Toast
- Vegan Chia Pudding with Berries
- Chocolate Chip Zucchini Bread

Avocado Toast with Cherry Tomatoes

Ingredients:

- 2 ripe avocados
- 4 slices of bread (whole grain or sourdough)
- 1 cup cherry tomatoes, halved
- Salt and pepper to taste
- Optional: red pepper flakes, lemon juice, fresh basil

Instructions:

1. **Toast the Bread:** Toast slices of bread until golden.
2. **Prepare the Avocado:** Mash avocados in a bowl, seasoning with salt, pepper, and lemon juice.
3. **Assemble:** Spread avocado on toast, top with cherry tomatoes, and garnish with red pepper flakes or basil if desired.

Quinoa Breakfast Bowl

Ingredients:

- 1 cup cooked quinoa
- 1/2 cup almond milk (or any milk)
- 1 tablespoon honey or maple syrup
- 1/2 teaspoon cinnamon
- Toppings: nuts, seeds, berries, banana slices

Instructions:

1. **Mix Ingredients:** In a bowl, combine cooked quinoa, almond milk, honey, and cinnamon.
2. **Serve:** Top with your choice of nuts, seeds, and fresh fruit.

Chia Seed Pudding

Ingredients:

- 1/2 cup chia seeds
- 2 cups almond milk (or any milk)
- 2 tablespoons maple syrup or honey
- 1 teaspoon vanilla extract
- Toppings: fresh fruit, nuts, granola

Instructions:

1. **Combine Ingredients:** In a bowl, whisk together chia seeds, almond milk, maple syrup, and vanilla.
2. **Refrigerate:** Let sit for at least 4 hours or overnight until thickened.
3. **Serve:** Top with fruit and nuts before serving.

Smoothie Bowl with Granola

Ingredients:

- 1 banana, frozen
- 1 cup spinach or kale
- 1 cup almond milk (or any milk)
- Toppings: granola, sliced fruits, seeds, nut butter

Instructions:

1. **Blend:** In a blender, combine frozen banana, spinach, and almond milk until smooth.
2. **Serve:** Pour into a bowl and top with granola and your favorite toppings.

Oatmeal with Fresh Fruit

Ingredients:

- 1 cup rolled oats
- 2 cups water or milk
- Toppings: fresh fruit (banana, berries), nuts, honey, cinnamon

Instructions:

1. **Cook the Oats:** In a pot, bring water or milk to a boil. Stir in oats and reduce heat. Cook for 5-10 minutes until creamy.
2. **Serve:** Top with fresh fruit, nuts, honey, and cinnamon.

Banana Pancakes

Ingredients:

- 1 cup flour
- 1 tablespoon baking powder
- 1/4 teaspoon salt
- 1 cup milk
- 1 ripe banana, mashed
- 1 egg
- Optional: chocolate chips or nuts

Instructions:

1. **Mix Ingredients:** In a bowl, combine flour, baking powder, and salt. In another bowl, mix milk, banana, and egg. Combine both mixtures.
2. **Cook:** Heat a skillet over medium heat. Pour batter onto skillet and cook until bubbles form, then flip and cook until golden.

Greek Yogurt Parfait

Ingredients:

- 2 cups Greek yogurt
- 1 cup granola
- 1 cup mixed berries (strawberries, blueberries, raspberries)
- Honey or maple syrup (optional)

Instructions:

1. **Layer Ingredients:** In a glass or bowl, layer Greek yogurt, granola, and berries.
2. **Drizzle:** Add honey or syrup if desired. Repeat layers and serve.

Breakfast Burrito with Veggies

Ingredients:

- 4 large eggs
- 1/2 cup bell peppers, diced
- 1/2 cup spinach
- 1/4 cup onion, diced
- 4 tortillas
- Salt and pepper to taste
- Optional: cheese, salsa, avocado

Instructions:

1. **Cook Veggies:** In a skillet, sauté onion, bell peppers, and spinach until soft.
2. **Scramble Eggs:** Add eggs to the skillet, season with salt and pepper, and scramble until cooked.
3. **Assemble Burritos:** Fill tortillas with egg mixture, adding cheese or toppings if desired. Roll and serve.

Sweet Potato Hash

Ingredients:

- 2 sweet potatoes, diced
- 1 bell pepper, diced
- 1 onion, diced
- 2 tablespoons olive oil
- Salt and pepper to taste
- Optional: eggs for topping

Instructions:

1. **Cook Sweet Potatoes:** In a skillet, heat olive oil over medium heat. Add sweet potatoes and cook for about 10 minutes until tender.
2. **Add Veggies:** Stir in bell pepper and onion. Cook until softened and slightly charred.
3. **Serve:** Season with salt and pepper. Top with fried or poached eggs if desired.

Enjoy your delicious breakfasts!

Muesli with Nuts and Dried Fruit

Ingredients:

- 1 cup rolled oats
- 1/2 cup mixed nuts (almonds, walnuts, pecans)
- 1/2 cup dried fruit (raisins, apricots, cranberries)
- 1/4 cup yogurt or milk
- Honey or maple syrup (optional)

Instructions:

1. **Mix Ingredients:** In a bowl, combine rolled oats, nuts, and dried fruit.
2. **Serve:** Add yogurt or milk and drizzle with honey or maple syrup if desired.

Overnight Oats with Almond Butter

Ingredients:

- 1 cup rolled oats
- 1 cup almond milk (or any milk)
- 2 tablespoons almond butter
- 1 tablespoon chia seeds
- 1 tablespoon honey or maple syrup
- Toppings: fresh fruit, nuts

Instructions:

1. **Combine Ingredients:** In a jar or bowl, mix oats, almond milk, almond butter, chia seeds, and sweetener.
2. **Refrigerate:** Cover and refrigerate overnight.
3. **Serve:** Top with fresh fruit and nuts in the morning.

Breakfast Tacos with Salsa

Ingredients:

- 4 small tortillas
- 4 eggs
- 1/2 cup diced bell peppers
- 1/4 cup onion, diced
- Salt and pepper to taste
- Salsa for topping

Instructions:

1. **Cook Veggies:** In a skillet, sauté bell peppers and onion until soft.
2. **Scramble Eggs:** Add eggs to the skillet, season with salt and pepper, and scramble until cooked.
3. **Assemble Tacos:** Fill tortillas with egg mixture and top with salsa.

Coconut Rice Pudding

Ingredients:

- 1 cup cooked rice
- 1 can (13.5 oz) coconut milk
- 1/4 cup sugar
- 1 teaspoon vanilla extract
- Toppings: toasted coconut, fresh fruit, nuts

Instructions:

1. **Combine Ingredients:** In a saucepan, mix cooked rice, coconut milk, sugar, and vanilla. Heat over medium until warm.
2. **Serve:** Spoon into bowls and top with toasted coconut and fresh fruit.

Berry Muffins

Ingredients:

- 1 1/2 cups flour
- 1/2 cup sugar
- 1 tablespoon baking powder
- 1/2 teaspoon salt
- 1/2 cup milk
- 1/3 cup vegetable oil
- 1 egg
- 1 cup mixed berries (fresh or frozen)

Instructions:

1. **Preheat Oven:** Preheat oven to 375°F (190°C). Grease or line a muffin tin.
2. **Mix Dry Ingredients:** In a bowl, combine flour, sugar, baking powder, and salt.
3. **Mix Wet Ingredients:** In another bowl, whisk together milk, oil, and egg. Combine both mixtures and fold in berries.
4. **Bake:** Fill muffin cups and bake for 20-25 minutes until golden.

Frittata with Spinach and Feta

Ingredients:

- 6 eggs
- 1 cup spinach, chopped
- 1/2 cup feta cheese, crumbled
- 1/4 cup milk
- Salt and pepper to taste
- Olive oil for cooking

Instructions:

1. **Preheat Oven:** Preheat oven to 375°F (190°C).
2. **Mix Ingredients:** In a bowl, whisk together eggs, milk, salt, and pepper. Stir in spinach and feta.
3. **Cook:** Heat olive oil in an oven-safe skillet. Pour in egg mixture and cook for a few minutes until edges set.
4. **Bake:** Transfer skillet to oven and bake for 15-20 minutes until set. Slice and serve.

Smoothie with Spinach and Pineapple

Ingredients:

- 1 cup spinach
- 1 cup frozen pineapple chunks
- 1 banana
- 1 cup almond milk (or any milk)
- Optional: protein powder or flaxseeds

Instructions:

1. **Blend Ingredients:** In a blender, combine spinach, pineapple, banana, and almond milk. Blend until smooth.
2. **Serve:** Pour into a glass and enjoy!

Savory Oatmeal with Cheese

Ingredients:

- 1 cup rolled oats
- 2 cups water or broth
- 1/2 cup shredded cheese (cheddar or your choice)
- Salt and pepper to taste
- Optional toppings: sautéed veggies, a fried egg

Instructions:

1. **Cook Oats:** In a pot, bring water or broth to a boil. Stir in oats and cook until creamy.
2. **Mix in Cheese:** Stir in shredded cheese, salt, and pepper.
3. **Serve:** Top with sautéed veggies or a fried egg if desired.

Tofu Scramble with Veggies

Ingredients:

- 1 block firm tofu, drained and crumbled
- 1 cup mixed vegetables (bell peppers, spinach, onions)
- 1 tablespoon nutritional yeast (optional)
- 1 teaspoon turmeric
- Salt and pepper to taste
- Olive oil for cooking

Instructions:

1. **Cook Veggies:** In a skillet, heat olive oil and sauté vegetables until soft.
2. **Add Tofu:** Stir in crumbled tofu, nutritional yeast, turmeric, salt, and pepper. Cook for 5-7 minutes until heated through.
3. **Serve:** Enjoy as is or in a wrap.

Enjoy your delicious and nutritious breakfasts!

Fruit Salad with Mint

Ingredients:

- 2 cups mixed fresh fruit (berries, melons, kiwi, etc.)
- 1 tablespoon honey (optional)
- 1 tablespoon fresh mint, chopped
- Juice of 1 lime

Instructions:

1. **Combine Ingredients:** In a bowl, mix the fruit, honey, mint, and lime juice.
2. **Serve:** Toss gently and serve chilled.

Whole Wheat Banana Bread

Ingredients:

- 2 cups whole wheat flour
- 1 teaspoon baking soda
- 1/2 teaspoon salt
- 1/2 cup sugar or honey
- 1/2 cup melted coconut oil or butter
- 2 ripe bananas, mashed
- 2 eggs
- 1 teaspoon vanilla extract

Instructions:

1. **Preheat Oven:** Preheat oven to 350°F (175°C). Grease a loaf pan.
2. **Mix Dry Ingredients:** In a bowl, combine flour, baking soda, and salt.
3. **Mix Wet Ingredients:** In another bowl, whisk together sugar, oil, bananas, eggs, and vanilla.
4. **Combine:** Mix wet and dry ingredients until just combined. Pour into the loaf pan.
5. **Bake:** Bake for 50-60 minutes until a toothpick comes out clean. Let cool before slicing.

Breakfast Quinoa with Maple Syrup

Ingredients:

- 1 cup cooked quinoa
- 1 cup almond milk (or any milk)
- 2 tablespoons maple syrup
- 1/2 teaspoon vanilla extract
- Toppings: fresh fruit, nuts, seeds

Instructions:

1. **Combine Ingredients:** In a saucepan, mix quinoa, almond milk, maple syrup, and vanilla. Heat gently.
2. **Serve:** Spoon into bowls and top with fruit and nuts.

Cinnamon Roll Overnight Oats

Ingredients:

- 1 cup rolled oats
- 1 cup milk (dairy or plant-based)
- 2 tablespoons yogurt (optional)
- 1 tablespoon maple syrup
- 1 teaspoon cinnamon
- Toppings: chopped pecans, raisins, or cream cheese drizzle

Instructions:

1. **Mix Ingredients:** In a jar or bowl, combine oats, milk, yogurt, maple syrup, and cinnamon.
2. **Refrigerate:** Cover and refrigerate overnight.
3. **Serve:** Top with chopped pecans, raisins, or a drizzle of cream cheese.

Zucchini Fritters

Ingredients:

- 2 cups grated zucchini
- 1/2 cup flour (whole wheat or all-purpose)
- 1/4 cup grated cheese (optional)
- 2 eggs
- 1 teaspoon garlic powder
- Salt and pepper to taste
- Olive oil for cooking

Instructions:

1. **Prep Zucchini:** Squeeze out excess moisture from grated zucchini using a clean kitchen towel.
2. **Mix Ingredients:** In a bowl, combine zucchini, flour, cheese, eggs, garlic powder, salt, and pepper.
3. **Cook Fritters:** Heat olive oil in a skillet over medium heat. Drop spoonfuls of the mixture into the skillet and cook until golden brown on both sides.
4. **Serve:** Enjoy warm with yogurt or salsa.

Almond Flour Waffles

Ingredients:

- 2 cups almond flour
- 2 eggs
- 1/4 cup almond milk (or any milk)
- 1 tablespoon honey or maple syrup
- 1 teaspoon baking powder
- 1/2 teaspoon vanilla extract

Instructions:

1. **Preheat Waffle Maker:** Preheat your waffle maker according to the manufacturer's instructions.
2. **Mix Ingredients:** In a bowl, whisk together almond flour, eggs, almond milk, honey, baking powder, and vanilla until smooth.
3. **Cook Waffles:** Pour batter into the preheated waffle maker and cook until golden brown.
4. **Serve:** Serve with syrup, fruit, or yogurt.

Rice Cakes with Nut Butter and Bananas

Ingredients:

- Rice cakes
- Nut butter (peanut, almond, or your choice)
- 1 banana, sliced
- Optional toppings: honey, cinnamon, chia seeds

Instructions:

1. **Assemble:** Spread nut butter on rice cakes and top with banana slices.
2. **Add Toppings:** Drizzle with honey or sprinkle with cinnamon and chia seeds if desired.

Bagel with Lox and Cream Cheese

Ingredients:

- 2 bagels, halved
- 4 ounces cream cheese
- 8 ounces lox (smoked salmon)
- 1/2 red onion, thinly sliced
- Capers and fresh dill (optional)

Instructions:

1. **Toast Bagels:** Toast bagel halves until golden.
2. **Spread Cream Cheese:** Generously spread cream cheese on each half.
3. **Top:** Add lox, red onion, capers, and dill if desired. Serve immediately.

Enjoy your delicious and nutritious breakfast options!

Cauliflower Grits

Ingredients:

- 1 head cauliflower, chopped into florets
- 1 cup vegetable broth
- 1/4 cup nutritional yeast (optional)
- Salt and pepper to taste
- Optional toppings: cheese, green onions, or bacon

Instructions:

1. **Steam Cauliflower:** Steam cauliflower florets until tender.
2. **Blend:** In a blender, combine steamed cauliflower, vegetable broth, nutritional yeast, salt, and pepper. Blend until smooth.
3. **Serve:** Heat in a pot if needed and top with desired toppings.

French Toast Casserole

Ingredients:

- 1 loaf of bread, cubed (about 10 cups)
- 6 eggs
- 2 cups milk
- 1/2 cup sugar
- 1 teaspoon vanilla extract
- 1 teaspoon cinnamon
- Optional: maple syrup, berries for serving

Instructions:

1. **Preheat Oven:** Preheat oven to 350°F (175°C). Grease a baking dish.
2. **Mix Ingredients:** In a bowl, whisk together eggs, milk, sugar, vanilla, and cinnamon. Pour over bread cubes and mix well.
3. **Bake:** Bake for 30-40 minutes until golden and set. Serve with maple syrup and berries.

Polenta with Eggs and Tomato

Ingredients:

- 1 cup polenta
- 4 cups water or broth
- 4 eggs
- 1 can diced tomatoes (15 oz)
- Olive oil, salt, and pepper

Instructions:

1. **Cook Polenta:** In a pot, bring water or broth to a boil. Gradually whisk in polenta and cook until thickened, about 15 minutes. Season with salt and pepper.
2. **Prepare Eggs:** In a skillet, heat olive oil and fry eggs to your liking.
3. **Serve:** Spoon polenta into bowls, top with diced tomatoes and a fried egg.

Savory Scones with Cheese and Chives

Ingredients:

- 2 cups flour
- 1 tablespoon baking powder
- 1/2 teaspoon salt
- 1/4 cup butter, cold and cubed
- 1 cup shredded cheese (cheddar or your choice)
- 1/4 cup chopped chives
- 3/4 cup milk

Instructions:

1. **Preheat Oven:** Preheat oven to 400°F (200°C). Line a baking sheet with parchment paper.
2. **Mix Dry Ingredients:** In a bowl, combine flour, baking powder, and salt. Cut in butter until crumbly.
3. **Add Cheese and Chives:** Stir in cheese and chives. Add milk and mix until combined.
4. **Shape and Bake:** Turn dough onto a floured surface, pat into a circle, and cut into wedges. Bake for 15-20 minutes until golden.

Vegan Breakfast Bowl

Ingredients:

- 1 cup cooked quinoa or brown rice
- 1/2 avocado, sliced
- 1/2 cup black beans, rinsed
- 1/2 cup cherry tomatoes, halved
- 1/4 cup corn (fresh or canned)
- Lime juice, cilantro, salt, and pepper

Instructions:

1. **Combine Ingredients:** In a bowl, layer quinoa or rice, black beans, avocado, cherry tomatoes, and corn.
2. **Season:** Drizzle with lime juice, sprinkle with cilantro, salt, and pepper. Serve warm or cold.

Puffed Rice with Dried Fruit

Ingredients:

- 3 cups puffed rice
- 1/2 cup dried fruit (raisins, apricots, etc.)
- 1/4 cup nuts or seeds (optional)
- 1/4 cup honey or maple syrup
- 1/2 teaspoon cinnamon

Instructions:

1. **Combine Ingredients:** In a large bowl, mix puffed rice, dried fruit, nuts, honey, and cinnamon.
2. **Serve:** Enjoy as is or with milk.

Cornmeal Pancakes

Ingredients:

- 1 cup cornmeal
- 1 cup milk
- 1 egg
- 1 teaspoon baking powder
- 1 tablespoon sugar
- Salt to taste

Instructions:

1. **Mix Ingredients:** In a bowl, combine cornmeal, milk, egg, baking powder, sugar, and salt until smooth.
2. **Cook Pancakes:** Heat a skillet over medium heat and pour in batter. Cook until bubbles form, then flip and cook until golden.

Apple Cinnamon Breakfast Bake

Ingredients:

- 3 cups diced apples
- 1 cup rolled oats
- 1/2 cup milk
- 1/4 cup honey or maple syrup
- 1 teaspoon cinnamon
- 1/2 teaspoon baking powder
- Optional: nuts or raisins

Instructions:

1. **Preheat Oven:** Preheat oven to 350°F (175°C). Grease a baking dish.
2. **Combine Ingredients:** In a bowl, mix apples, oats, milk, sweetener, cinnamon, and baking powder. Stir in nuts or raisins if desired.
3. **Bake:** Pour into the baking dish and bake for 30-35 minutes until set.

Savory Oatmeal with Mushrooms

Ingredients:

- 1 cup rolled oats
- 2 cups water or broth
- 1 cup mushrooms, sliced
- 1 tablespoon olive oil
- Salt and pepper to taste
- Optional toppings: fried egg, green onions

Instructions:

1. **Cook Oats:** In a pot, bring water or broth to a boil. Stir in oats and cook until creamy.
2. **Sauté Mushrooms:** In a skillet, heat olive oil and sauté mushrooms until golden. Season with salt and pepper.
3. **Serve:** Spoon oatmeal into bowls, top with sautéed mushrooms and optional fried egg.

Enjoy these delicious breakfast options!

Breakfast Couscous with Almonds

Ingredients:

- 1 cup couscous
- 1 cup water or milk
- 1/4 cup sliced almonds
- 1 tablespoon honey or maple syrup
- Fresh fruit (berries, banana, etc.)
- Optional: cinnamon

Instructions:

1. **Cook Couscous:** Bring water or milk to a boil. Stir in couscous, cover, and remove from heat. Let sit for 5 minutes.
2. **Fluff and Serve:** Fluff with a fork, then stir in almonds, honey, and optional cinnamon. Top with fresh fruit.

Egg and Avocado Breakfast Sandwich

Ingredients:

- 2 slices whole grain bread
- 1 ripe avocado
- 2 eggs
- Salt and pepper to taste
- Optional: hot sauce, spinach, or tomato slices

Instructions:

1. **Toast Bread:** Toast the bread slices.
2. **Cook Eggs:** Fry or poach eggs to your liking.
3. **Assemble:** Mash avocado onto one slice of bread, season with salt and pepper, add eggs, and top with any optional ingredients. Close sandwich and serve.

Smoked Salmon and Avocado Salad

Ingredients:

- 4 ounces smoked salmon
- 1 ripe avocado, diced
- 2 cups mixed greens
- 1/2 red onion, thinly sliced
- Juice of 1 lemon
- Olive oil, salt, and pepper

Instructions:

1. **Combine Ingredients:** In a bowl, mix smoked salmon, avocado, mixed greens, and red onion.
2. **Dress Salad:** Drizzle with lemon juice, olive oil, salt, and pepper. Toss gently and serve.

Peanut Butter Banana Smoothie

Ingredients:

- 1 banana
- 2 tablespoons peanut butter
- 1 cup almond milk (or any milk)
- 1 tablespoon honey (optional)
- Ice cubes (optional)

Instructions:

1. **Blend Ingredients:** In a blender, combine banana, peanut butter, almond milk, and honey. Add ice for a colder smoothie.
2. **Serve:** Blend until smooth and pour into a glass.

Berry Chia Jam on Toast

Ingredients:

- 1 cup mixed berries (fresh or frozen)
- 2 tablespoons chia seeds
- 1 tablespoon honey or maple syrup
- Bread for toasting

Instructions:

1. **Cook Berries:** In a saucepan, cook berries over medium heat until they break down. Stir in chia seeds and sweetener.
2. **Thicken:** Simmer for a few minutes until thickened.
3. **Serve:** Spread on toasted bread and enjoy.

Spinach and Mushroom Quiche

Ingredients:

- 1 pie crust (store-bought or homemade)
- 4 eggs
- 1 cup milk
- 2 cups fresh spinach, chopped
- 1 cup mushrooms, sliced
- 1 cup shredded cheese (cheddar or your choice)
- Salt and pepper to taste

Instructions:

1. **Preheat Oven:** Preheat oven to 375°F (190°C).
2. **Sauté Vegetables:** In a skillet, sauté mushrooms until tender, then add spinach until wilted.
3. **Mix Ingredients:** In a bowl, whisk eggs and milk. Stir in sautéed veggies, cheese, salt, and pepper.
4. **Bake:** Pour mixture into pie crust and bake for 30-35 minutes until set. Let cool before slicing.

Sweet Potato Pancakes

Ingredients:

- 1 cup mashed sweet potatoes
- 1 cup flour (whole wheat or all-purpose)
- 1 teaspoon baking powder
- 1 teaspoon cinnamon
- 2 eggs
- 1/2 cup milk
- Optional: maple syrup for serving

Instructions:

1. **Mix Ingredients:** In a bowl, combine sweet potatoes, flour, baking powder, cinnamon, eggs, and milk until smooth.
2. **Cook Pancakes:** Heat a skillet over medium heat and pour in batter. Cook until bubbles form, then flip and cook until golden.
3. **Serve:** Serve with maple syrup if desired.

Cacao Nib Granola

Ingredients:

- 2 cups rolled oats
- 1/2 cup nuts (almonds, walnuts, etc.)
- 1/4 cup cacao nibs
- 1/4 cup honey or maple syrup
- 1/4 cup coconut oil, melted
- 1/2 teaspoon vanilla extract
- Pinch of salt

Instructions:

1. **Preheat Oven:** Preheat oven to 350°F (175°C). Line a baking sheet with parchment paper.
2. **Mix Ingredients:** In a bowl, combine oats, nuts, cacao nibs, honey, coconut oil, vanilla, and salt.
3. **Bake:** Spread mixture on the baking sheet and bake for 20-25 minutes, stirring halfway through until golden. Let cool and store in an airtight container.

Enjoy these delicious breakfast options!

Toasted Coconut Granola

Ingredients:

- 2 cups rolled oats
- 1 cup shredded coconut
- 1/2 cup nuts (almonds, walnuts, etc.)
- 1/4 cup honey or maple syrup
- 1/4 cup coconut oil, melted
- 1/2 teaspoon vanilla extract
- Pinch of salt

Instructions:

1. **Preheat Oven:** Preheat oven to 350°F (175°C). Line a baking sheet with parchment paper.
2. **Mix Ingredients:** In a bowl, combine oats, coconut, nuts, honey, coconut oil, vanilla, and salt.
3. **Bake:** Spread mixture on the baking sheet and bake for 20-25 minutes, stirring halfway, until golden. Let cool and store in an airtight container.

Matcha Overnight Oats

Ingredients:

- 1 cup rolled oats
- 1 cup almond milk (or any milk)
- 1 tablespoon matcha powder
- 1 tablespoon chia seeds
- 1 tablespoon honey or maple syrup
- Toppings: fresh fruit, nuts

Instructions:

1. **Combine Ingredients:** In a jar or bowl, mix oats, almond milk, matcha powder, chia seeds, and sweetener.
2. **Refrigerate:** Cover and refrigerate overnight.
3. **Serve:** Stir well in the morning and top with fruit and nuts.

Spicy Avocado Salsa on Toast

Ingredients:

- 1 ripe avocado
- 1 small tomato, diced
- 1/2 red onion, diced
- 1 jalapeño, seeded and minced (optional)
- Juice of 1 lime
- Salt and pepper to taste
- Bread for toasting

Instructions:

1. **Mash Avocado:** In a bowl, mash avocado and mix in tomato, onion, jalapeño, lime juice, salt, and pepper.
2. **Serve:** Spread on toasted bread and enjoy.

Breakfast Ramen with Soft-Boiled Egg

Ingredients:

- 2 packages instant ramen noodles
- 4 cups vegetable broth
- 2 eggs
- 1 cup spinach or bok choy
- Green onions for garnish
- Soy sauce or miso paste (optional)

Instructions:

1. **Cook Eggs:** In a pot, boil water and gently add eggs. Boil for 6-7 minutes, then transfer to an ice bath. Peel once cooled.
2. **Prepare Ramen:** In another pot, bring vegetable broth to a boil. Add ramen noodles and cook according to package instructions. Stir in spinach at the end.
3. **Serve:** Divide noodles and broth into bowls, top with halved eggs, and garnish with green onions.

Ricotta and Honey Toast

Ingredients:

- 2 slices whole grain bread
- 1/2 cup ricotta cheese
- 2 tablespoons honey
- Optional toppings: nuts, fruit, or cinnamon

Instructions:

1. **Toast Bread:** Toast the bread slices until golden.
2. **Assemble:** Spread ricotta cheese on each slice, drizzle with honey, and add any optional toppings.
3. **Serve:** Enjoy immediately.

Vegan Chia Pudding with Berries

Ingredients:

- 1/4 cup chia seeds
- 1 cup almond milk (or any plant-based milk)
- 1 tablespoon maple syrup or agave (optional)
- Fresh berries for topping

Instructions:

1. **Mix Ingredients:** In a bowl, whisk together chia seeds, almond milk, and sweetener.
2. **Refrigerate:** Let sit for 10 minutes, stir, and then refrigerate for at least 2 hours or overnight.
3. **Serve:** Top with fresh berries before serving.

Chocolate Chip Zucchini Bread

Ingredients:

- 1 1/2 cups grated zucchini (about 1 medium zucchini)
- 1 1/2 cups flour
- 1/2 cup sugar
- 1/2 cup brown sugar
- 1/2 cup vegetable oil
- 2 eggs
- 1 teaspoon vanilla extract
- 1 teaspoon baking soda
- 1/2 teaspoon baking powder
- 1/2 teaspoon salt
- 1/2 cup chocolate chips

Instructions:

1. **Preheat Oven:** Preheat oven to 350°F (175°C). Grease a loaf pan.
2. **Mix Wet Ingredients:** In a bowl, combine grated zucchini, sugars, oil, eggs, and vanilla.
3. **Mix Dry Ingredients:** In another bowl, whisk together flour, baking soda, baking powder, and salt. Gradually add dry ingredients to wet mixture.
4. **Add Chocolate Chips:** Fold in chocolate chips. Pour batter into the loaf pan.
5. **Bake:** Bake for 50-60 minutes until a toothpick comes out clean. Let cool before slicing.

Enjoy these delightful breakfast options!

www.ingramcontent.com/pod-product-compliance
Lightning Source LLC
LaVergne TN
LVHW081331060526
838201LV00055B/2584